RICHARD WOFF

• • •

Explore the
British Museum
A family souvenir guide

THE BRITISH MUSEUM PRESS

Welcome to the world of
The British Museum!

The museum was founded in 1753 and celebrated its 250th birthday in 2003. It was the first publicly-owned museum in the world and was intended to be used by everybody, free of charge.

At the time of the Museum's founding, European thinkers were making great changes in their understanding of the world. They were questioning traditional ideas, taking more time to observe nature and human behaviour and recognising the huge variety of human cultures. The power of the British empire meant that traders, explorers, scientists, generals and admirals brought to the Museum all sorts of objects for scholars to study.

Today, artists, designers, craftspeople and many others still come to the British Museum for inspiration. The Museum still contains and collects objects from every period of human history and every part of the globe. Every year millions of people from all around the world come to visit or study or to help the Museum understand better the objects from their cultures. Members of Museum staff help colleagues in museums abroad to protect, study and display their collections. Every year thousands of objects from the Museum travel the continents – sometimes back to the countries from which they came, sometimes to countries that have no examples of those objects in their own museums. The British Museum has become a museum of the world for the world. We hope that you enjoy exploring the Museum and that the chance you have here to see objects from different countries alongside each other will help you understand better the fascinating variety of world cultures, the connections between them and what human beings have in common.

How to use this guide

The guide contains nine objects which are highlights of the British Museum. Each object connects to a theme that leads to six or seven other objects linked to the theme.

You could decide to go and see the nine highlights. Or you could decide to visit one or two highlights plus their connected objects. Or you could just pick the objects at random!

All the highlights and most of the other objects in the guide are usually on display in the Museum. We show their room numbers, and the map on the back cover of this book will show you how to find the rooms.

WARNING!

Sometimes rooms have to be closed, and sometimes we lend objects to other museums or move them to different parts of the main Museum. Sometimes objects have to be cleaned or rested – some sorts of objects are affected by light so they cannot remain on display for long periods. This means that you may not be able to find all the objects at one visit. We are sorry if this happens, but are sure you will find lots of other fascinating things to visit instead!

Things to do

Pick up one of our family leaflets at the Information Desk to find out about all the different things you can do. If you visit the Museum during a school holiday you will probably find free events that you can join in. We bring in artists, storytellers, musicians and dancers to help you to enjoy your visit and to understand more about the cultures from which our objects come. But no matter when you come we have things you can do. Just go along to the Hamlyn Library and you can collect free trails on different parts of the Museum, for example, Egypt, Greece and Africa, and free activity backpacks with games, puzzles and other things to do in the galleries. You can also read books in our children's library and visit our website to find out more about what you have seen.

If you want to explore the Museum after you get home or before you come, visit **www.britishmuseum.org** Click on Explore to find the children's section, which has lots of information and activities. We also have some fantastic interactive websites which are great to help with homework or just to explore:
www.ancientegypt.co.uk
www.ancientgreece.co.uk
www.ancientchina.co.uk
www.earlyimperialchina.co.uk
www.mesopotamia.co.uk
www.ancientindia.co.uk
www.mughalindia.co.uk
www.ancientcivilizations.co.uk

Young Friends of the British Museum

As a Young Friend you can get closer to the British Museum and enjoy some fantastic benefits for just £20 a year.

Five sleepovers a year. Spend the night exploring the Museum after dark!

Receive our children's magazine, **remus**, three times a year.

Plus there's a wide variety of events for you and your family to enjoy. And you'll get a great membership pack when you join.

**To join call us today on +44 (0)20 7323 8195
or visit us online at
www.britishmuseum.org/join_in/membership.aspx**
Registered Charity Number 1086080

Children taking part in an Aztec activity at one of the Museum's holiday events.

The Rosetta Stone

What is it?

A broken part of a granite block called a stela.

How old is it?

It was set up in 196 BC.

Where did it come from?

It was found at the village of Rashid, or Rosetta, in Egypt, but was probably first set up at the nearby city of Sais.

What was it for?

It was set up in honour of King Ptolemy V.

How heavy is it?

Around 762 kg. It was too heavy for the floors of the original Museum's buildings when it arrived here.

Where can I see it?

Room 4, the Egyptian sculpture gallery. There is also a replica of the Stone that you can touch in Room 1, the Enlightment Gallery.

This is the most famous single object in the British Museum, not because it is beautiful or old, but because of what is written on it. An announcement has been carved on to the Stone three times. At the bottom it is in ancient Greek – at the time the Stone was carved, Egypt was ruled by Greek kings and queens. In the middle it is in Ancient Egyptian, in a kind of everyday writing called Demotic. At the top, the announcement is in Ancient Egyptian in picture-like hieroglyphs.

In summer 1799, when the Rosetta Stone was found by Napoleon Bonaparte's army, nobody had known how to read hieroglyphs or Demotic for over a thousand years. Egypt seemed a strange and mysterious land, with its huge sculptures and incredibly preserved mummies. Unlike other ancient peoples such as the Romans or Greeks, the ancient Egyptians could not make themselves heard in their own words.

Scholars realised the importance of having the writing in both Egyptian and Greek. Copies of the Stone were made and sent round to European scholars who were trying to decipher hieroglyphs. The man who made the breakthrough was Jean-François Champollion. He realised that the hieroglyphic signs were not simple picture-writing, but also stood for sounds, just as English letters do, and that they wrote the ancient Egyptian language. Experts are still studying Ancient Egyptian texts, but since Champollion published his work in 1822 the people of ancient Egypt have been able to speak directly to us after a long silence. Because of this, the Rosetta Stone has become a symbol of all our attempts to understand the past in its own words.

When it first arrived in the Museum, the Stone was displayed at an angle in a special iron cradle, but in 2004 Museum conservators cleaned the Stone carefully and put it upright and now it stands up perfectly without any help.

Why is the Rosetta Stone here?

The Rosetta Stone was found when Napoleon invaded Egypt. By 1801, the British defeated the French, who were forced to give up the antiquities their scholars had collected to the British. These included the Rosetta Stone, which came to the Museum in 1802.

So what does it actually say?

The announcement is from a gathering of priests in the city of Memphis. They list many achievements of the king – who was only thirteen at the time – such as victories in battle. In return for gifts of grain and money and lower taxes on their temples, the priests proclaim Ptolemy to be a god and declare that daily rituals and a yearly festival should be carried out to worship him.

Writing

Without the Rosetta Stone we might never have been able to understand the writing of the ancient Egyptians. Look closely in the galleries of the Museum and you will see writing everywhere.

Like Egyptian hieroglyphs, the small pictures on this carving from the Maya people in Mexico are a mixture of picture-writing and sounds. Most Maya inscriptions record dates and events such as battles, religious rituals and family trees. These showed that the Maya rulers had carried out their duties and were entitled to be rulers.

Room 27

Room 49

In contrast, the people who wrote on these thin strips of wood never intended that they would survive long. The tablets were preserved by accident in boggy land at the Roman fort of Vindolanda, near Hadrian's Wall. They give us a vivid glimpse of everyday life in Roman Britain: who was on guard duty, who had not turned up for work, that a mother was sending her son some new underpants, an invitation to a birthday party, a shopping list and what may perhaps be a child's homework.

The earliest writing in the world comes from the civilizations that grew up 6,000 years ago in the fertile land between the Tigris and Euphrates rivers in what is now Iraq. This writing was done by making marks in clay with a reed or stick and is called 'cuneiform'. Most cuneiform documents are official records from the palaces of kings, but some are letters and others are stories, including this one (right) the earliest version of a Flood story similar to that of Noah.

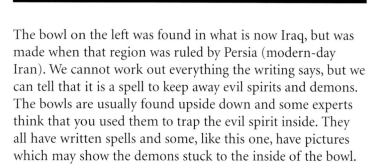

Room 55

Room 52

The bowl on the left was found in what is now Iraq, but was made when that region was ruled by Persia (modern-day Iran). We cannot work out everything the writing says, but we can tell that it is a spell to keep away evil spirits and demons. The bowls are usually found upside down and some experts think that you used them to trap the evil spirit inside. They all have written spells and some, like this one, have pictures which may show the demons stuck to the inside of the bowl.

Calligraphy is the art of making writing beautiful. This glass lamp was made for a mosque in Cairo in the fourteenth century AD. On it the calligrapher has written part of the Qur'an which compares the light of the lamp to the light of God. Not satisfied just with the meaning of the words, he has also made the writing beautiful so that it communicates the word and the beauty of God.

Room 34

2

A Greek drinking cup

What is it?

A wine cup made of pottery. It is painted with scenes showing a drinking party at which just such cups are being used.

How old is it?

It was made in about 485–480 BC, so it is nearly 2,500 years old.

Where did it come from?

It was found in Vulci, Italy, in an area that belonged to the Etruscan people, who were early inhabitants of Italy. It had been placed in a tomb as an offering to the dead person.

Who made it/used it?

It was actually made in Athens in Greece, and then sold to the Etruscans by traders. Athenian pottery was very popular and was traded all around the Mediterranean Sea.

Where can I see it?

Room 69, the gallery on ancient Greek and Roman daily life. It is on show together with other objects relating to Greek dining and drinking.

On the inside of the cup another man is painted holding a cup by its handle and a walking stick; he may already be on his way home – or to the next party!

At dinner parties, Greek men used to lie on couches to eat. When they had finished eating, they would start drinking wine from painted pottery cups like this one. On the outside of the cup, six men – three on each side – are shown at a party called a symposium (Greek for 'drinking together'). Young boys are refilling their cups from jugs. The couches were arranged around all four walls of a rectangular room and the artist has tried to show this by painting two of the couches end-on. In front of the couches you can also see low tables, one of which clearly has three legs (right).

Although the cup has two handles, most of the men at this symposium hold their cups by the bottom of the foot. The handles had two other purposes: one was so that the cups could be hung up on the wall – you can see cups and wine jugs hanging on the wall behind the drinkers. The second purpose was for playing a game called *kottabos*: swirling the cup by one handle, a man could throw the last drops of wine at a target.

Scenes on other pots show *kottabos* as well as other forms of entertainment including reciting poetry, playing music, singing and dancing. Sometimes parties got rowdy and arguments and even fights could break out.

Why are there no women at the party?

At an Athenian symposium, only men would get together, in a special room of the house set aside for symposia. Their wives or daughters would not be present but professional female musicians and dancers might be hired for the evening to entertain the men. Women were not normally meant to go out much or drink wine, although at special religious festivals they too held women-only parties.

Why did the Greeks use such large pottery cups and not smaller glasses for their wine?

Glass was not very common in ancient Greece as it was difficult to produce. Pottery, on the other hand, was made of clay that was available almost everywhere and was very sturdy. The Athenians were particularly good at making beautifully shaped cups covered with a shiny black paint and decorated with interesting scenes. They were also difficult to drink from, which meant that drinkers could show off their skills at using them elegantly – or would start to spill wine when they got too drunk!

Eating
and drinking

Everyone needs to eat and drink to stay alive, but food and meals are not always just a necessity. The galleries in the Museum show that the ancient Greeks were not the only people to turn eating and drinking into something special.

Room 41

Room 67

Wine was drunk in Korea as well as in Greece, but around the tenth century AD tea-drinking became popular. It was believed that tea tasted best when drunk from a green bowl like this one (left), which is decorated inside with a lotus flower. For an Anglo-Saxon chief and his attendants, ale would be the favourite drink and they would drink it from horns during feasts in the Great Hall. The huge horn above has been decorated with silver around the lip and tip.

If you were wealthy and important enough to be eating a meat stew in Ireland in the late Bronze Age (about 1050–900 BC), it is likely that the stew would be cooked in a large cauldron. The trick was to get out the chunks of meat and for that you might use a flesh hook. This one is finely decorated with ravens and swans and so probably belonged to a chief.

A rich Briton living in the late Roman period (4th century AD) could have had this magnificent silver dish laid out on the dining table. It was found in the east of England along with other silver dishes, bowls, plates, spoons and tableware. It is decorated with scenes featuring Bacchus the Roman god of wine. At the end of a dinner in 16th century England, the host might have sweets brought out on flat, circular wooden mats called trenchers. Once the guests had eaten the sweets, they could turn the trenchers over to find poems, sayings, puzzles and games that could keep them amused for hours.

Room 49

Room 46

Room 63

Food and drink are vital for life; for the ancient Egyptians they were just as vital for life after death. Models like this bakery were put in tombs to guarantee the dead person a plentiful supply of bread. The rows of workers are grinding the flour, sieving it, kneading the dough and baking the bread in circular ovens. For the ancient Chinese, it was important to carry out rituals to honour your ancestors so that they would speak with the gods on your behalf. Wealthy tombs contained superb bronze vessels so that the dead person could continue to offer food and drink to their ancestors.

Room 33

Room 51

11

3

Hoa Hakananai'a

What is it?

A stone statue from Rapa Nui (also called Easter Island), the most isolated inhabited island in the world, in the eastern Pacific Ocean.

How old is it?

It was one of hundreds of similar statues which were carved some time between AD 1000 and AD 1600.

What was it for?

It was made to stand on the temple-platform of a local clan, to represent their ancestral gods.

How did it get here?

In 1868 a British navy ship, HMS *Topaze*, visited Rapa Nui. Its officers, with the help of local leaders and missionaries, had Hoa Hakananai'a taken aboard. When they offered it to Queen Victoria, she told them to give it to the British Museum.

How big is it?

It is nearly 2.5 metres tall and weighs about 4 metric tonnes.

Where can I see it?

In the Wellcome Gallery, room 24.

Rapa Nui was settled more than a thousand years ago by Polynesian voyagers from islands to the west. Over a 400 year period, their descendants carved hundreds of statues like this and set them up on religious shrines and other places around the island. At first, Rapa Nui was rich in forests and in sea birds which the people hunted for food, but as the population grew, it used up these natural resources. Farming became difficult, food supplies scarce and local clans fought over land.

The clans threw down the statues of their enemies, but still joined in the important annual religious festival of the birdman at Orongo in the western corner of the island. This is where Hoa Hakananai'a comes from. When the British navy took him, they had to dig him out of the floor of a special stone-walled house which had been built around him.

Unlike most statues on Rapa Nui, Hoa Hakananai'a is carved on his back with birdmen and other religious symbols.

When European voyagers began visiting Rapa Nui in the 18th century, they were mystified by the huge stone statues. They could not imagine that the islanders could possibly have carved the great statues and moved them into place. Today there are still some who believe that people from other continents or even aliens from other worlds made them. However, researchers spoke to the islanders and carried out proper archaeological investigations to find out how the islanders did it. They used hard stone tools to carve the statues from soft volcanic rock and then dragged them into position and stood them up. Not long after the arrival of the first Europeans, others began capturing the islanders to work as slaves in Peru. Some of them managed to return, but brought with them diseases which wiped out most of the population.

Hoa Hakananai'a was clearly special among the many statues on Rapa Nui and he still is. Rapanuians have advised the British Museum how he should be displayed and have come to visit him and lay flowers around him.

What happened at the Orongo festival?

In the birdman ceremonies, the leading chiefs of the island each sent a swimmer over to a rocky islet off the southwest peninsula in a race to bring back the first egg of the year from the terns that nested there. The winning chief became birdman for the year, living representative of the creator god Makemake and a powerful figure among the various clans of the island.

A boulder with a carving of a birdman figure holding an egg.

Museum Mysteries

The British Museum's purpose is to help us understand and appreciate the cultures and achievements of peoples such as the inhabitants of Rapa Nui. However, there are still objects in the Museum about which we know very little and some questions we may never answer fully.

We know quite a lot about this bronze jug. It was made in the 14th century. It has a royal coat of arms and symbols which show that it was probably used in the household of King Richard II of England. But it was found in 1896 under a sacred tree in the palace of the king of the Asante people in what is now Ghana. How did this jug get from the palace of one king to the palace of another more than 3,000 miles away?

In about 2500–2600 BC, someone in Yorkshire buried these stone drums (below) with a dead child. At about the same time, this jade tube or 'cong' (opposite) was buried in a grave in China. We do not know what the drums and cong were for. They both suggest that the dead people were important or wealthy. The fact that congs have been found in many graves suggests that they may have some religious meaning. So far, no other stone drums have ever been found anywhere else.

Room 2

Room 51

Room 34

Room 51

These carved stone balls (right) are over 5,000 years old. More than four hundred have been found in Scotland, but not all in specific places like graves or houses so it is hard to judge what they may have been used for or what they meant to the people who owned them. The beautifully decorated object above is from India and is only three hundred years old. The ends unscrew to reveal sharp blades. Is it a pointer for reading holy books? Or a backscratcher? Or a secret weapon?

Room 24

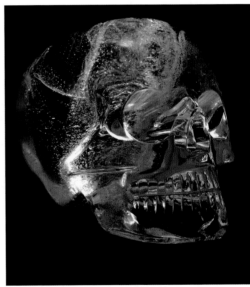

Room 33

For a long time it was thought that this crystal skull was a sacred religious object from the ancient Aztec culture. Using an electron-scanning microscope, scientists at the Museum discovered that the carved lines were made using a European jeweller's wheel, probably in the nineteenth century. In spite of this, there are people who still believe that the skull has a mysterious, magic power that scientific and archaeological evidence can never dispel.

The Lewis Chessmen

One of the queens, showing the fine carving on the back of her throne.

How many are there?

There are sixty-seven chessmen in total at the British Museum, and eleven more at the National Museum of Scotland in Edinburgh. They were found with fourteen counters and a belt buckle made of walrus ivory.

How old are they?

They were carved between about AD 1150 and AD 1200.

Where did they come from?

They were found in a sand dune on the Isle of Lewis in the Outer Hebrides, but were probably made in Norway.

Who made and owned them?

They were made in a workshop, perhaps by more than one carver. They were luxury products and were possibly being carried by a merchant travelling from Norway to Ireland.

What are they made of?

They were carved from walrus' tusks and whales' teeth.

Where can I see them?

In Room 40, the Medieval Europe gallery.

The Lewis chessmen are the most famous chessmen in the world. They were bought by the Museum from an Edinburgh dealer, T. A. Forrest, in November 1831 for 80 guineas. Forrest had already sold another 10 pieces privately which, together with a bishop which came to light later, were finally acquired by the National Museum of Scotland in 1880. It is still something of a mystery as to exactly how and where they were found and how Forrest came to have them.

The chessmen have not been dated scientifically because that would involve breaking a piece off one of them for analysis. However, we can date them stylistically by the way that the faces are carved and from the details of their dress. The knights are armed for battle according to the custom from about 1080 to AD 1200. The bishops, however, help us to be more precise about the dates. All of the bishops wear their mitres facing frontally, like modern-day bishops. This fashion did not come into practice until about 1150; therefore, we can be sure that the chessmen were made between about 1150 and 1200.

The chessmen represent the different ranks of society. The bishops, knights and infantrymen are ruled by a king and a queen. The kings and queens sit on ornamental thrones. The kings hold swords as a symbol of their power and the queens ponder important matters of state with their chins resting in their hands. Kings were mighty in the twelfth century, but queens were also very rich and powerful. Henry II's queen, Eleanor of Aquitaine, even took part in a rebellion against her husband.

So who played chess in those days?

Chess was probably invented in India in the sixth century AD and was originally a way of training young noblemen for battle. The game spread to Europe via Iran and by the eleventh century was popular with aristocrats throughout Europe. The quality of the carving of the Lewis chessmen and the material they are made from suggest that they were intended for very rich owners. The merchant carrying them probably had four complete sets of pieces so he stood to make a lot of money.

Gone crazy...

Some of the pieces show a special type of Scandinavian warrior. These are 'berserkers' who worked themselves up into a terrible fighting frenzy before battle. The berserkers among the Lewis chessmen are so wild they are biting their shields. Can you spot any berserkers among the figures on this page?

Rulers and royalty

The Lewis chess pieces range from ordinary people up to kings and queens. The British Museum is full of reminders of power and prestige.

Shyaam aMbul aNgoong, king of the Kuba, sits, ready to listen to his people. He wears belts, armlets, bracelets and a hat and carries a knife, all of which symbolize his royalty. His personal symbol is the board game in front of him. When a Kuba king was away, such statues kept his rule safe.

Room 25

This headdress was owned by Yellow Calf, the last chief of the Arapaho tribe. The feathers, taken from the tail of a golden eagle, were very hard to get when you weren't allowed to kill the bird. Each feather stands for an act of bravery in battle. Yellow Calf must have been a great warrior.

Room 26

Room 70   *Room 25*

Rulers need to show their faces to their subjects to remind them of their power. The bronze head of Augustus, the first Roman emperor, is part of an over-life-size statue from what is now Sudan, one of the farthest parts of the Roman Empire. The statue probably stood in a place where everyone could see it.

The bronze head of Queen Idia was made to be placed on an altar in the royal palace in Benin. In the early 1500s, Queen Idia helped her son, the Oba of Benin, to overcome his enemies and strengthen his rule. From that time on, Queen Mothers became very important in the royal household and were treated with great respect.

The jewel showing Queen Elizabeth I of England was probably given by Elizabeth to a member of her court to wear as a mark of their loyalty. Ordinary people could afford to wear the badge showing Queen Victoria. It was made to celebrate her sixty years on the throne and shows the queen in 1837 and in 1897. Portraits of Elizabeth I do not show her growing old.

Coins allow a ruler to spread their image far and wide in people's hands, purses and pockets. The third object looks like a coin, but it isn't, it's another badge. It shows the head of Jahangir, a Mughal emperor of India. Jahangir had these 'coins' made to be given away to devoted subjects who could wear them on their sashes and turbans.

Room 46

Temporarily off display

Temporarily off display

19

The Sutton Hoo helmet

What is it?

The remains of a man's iron helmet.

Where is it from?

It's from the boat burial in Mound 1 at Sutton Hoo in Suffolk in eastern England. It was found shattered into more than 500 pieces.

How old is it?

It was made in the late sixth or early seventh centuries AD. We think that it was probably buried at some point between about AD 595 and 640.

Who did it belong to?

The burial contained such valuable and beautifully-made objects that the dead person must have been very important, perhaps one of the East Anglian kings.

How heavy is it?

We estimate that it originally weighed about 2.5 kg.

How did it come to the BM?

Mrs Edith Pretty, who owned the Sutton Hoo estate, gave it to the Museum in 1939.

Where can I see it?

Room 41, the Sutton Hoo and early medieval gallery. The modern replica of the helmet is also on display.

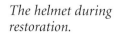

The helmet during restoration.

The Sutton Hoo helmet is one of the most famous objects from the early Anglo-Saxon era and one of the most famous objects ever found in England. It is an iron cap with a fixed face mask attached. The ear-flaps and neck-guard were attached with leather hinges. Once the ear-flaps were tied under the chin, the helmet protected its wearer's head completely. The helmet was intricately decorated and therefore it might have been for show, rather than for fighting. But as all the parts work properly it could keep the wearer safe from harm as well.

The cap was made by hammering up a single piece of iron into shape. The whole helmet was decorated with thin plates of bronze with pictures and patterns hammered through them, which were then covered in a layer of tin. They gave the helmet a silvery appearance. Over the top runs an iron crest inlaid with silver wire. Its ends are formed by animal heads cast in bronze covered in gold (gilt-bronze) with patterns punched in them and garnets for eyes. Two rows of red garnet stones follow the line of the eyebrows which end in boar's heads. The gilt-bronze nose, mouth and eyebrows are all inlaid with silver wires. These facial features form a flying bird or dragon: The moustache is the bird's tail, the nose its body and the eyebrows are the wings. Its head with garnet eyes goes snout-to-snout with the end of the iron crest.

When the complicated detail and beauty of the design emerged, scholars as well as the general public were astonished. So many different materials and sophisticated techniques had been used in creating the helmet, that it changed the way people looked at what were then called the 'Dark Ages' when life was thought to have been primitive and poor.

Protective pictures?

The stamped metal panels on the helmet include several different motifs. One panel shows two dancing warriors with helmets brandishing spears and swords. The exact meaning of these images is unknown. We think that they stood for skill in battle and might have had some protective purpose.

Models and inspirations

Some thirty similar helmets have been excavated in Scandinavia. Even if the Sutton Hoo helmet was made in England, the maker certainly knew the Scandinavian models. Perhaps he or at least some of his tools might have come from there. Scholars believe that this type of helmet was inspired by late Roman cavalry helmets which the north European metalworkers adapted to create their own, new style of helmet.

A modern replica of the helmet.

PROTECTION

Even if it was never worn in battle, the Sutton Hoo helmet was intended to protect its wearer. Throughout the Museum you can find objects designed to keep away danger and evil.

Room 69

It may seem natural that a gladiator in ancient Rome needed a helmet to protect his head, but gladiator contests were not that straightforward. The fighter who wore this type of heavy helmet also wore thick arm guards and bronze greaves on his legs and carried a short stabbing sword. The problem was that he had to fight a quick, lightly-armed opponent who could strike from a distance. So what price this sort of protection?

The Samurai warriors of Japan traditionally favoured bows and swords as weapons so their armour needed to protect them from arrows and from cutting blows. The suit covers almost the whole body and is made from small overlapping steel plates which made the armour flexible and allowed the wearer to move easily. But this suit has something else – a thick body plate to protect the warrior from bullets!

Room 93

Room 68

Throughout history and all around the world, people have protected themselves from evil by using powerful charms or amulets. Sometimes the protection comes from the form of the amulet and what it stands for – such as an eye or a cross. Sometimes the protective power comes from the material it is made from and its colour. These are just a few of the amulets on display in the Museum: Japanese coin amulets, an Egyptian *wedjat* eye, an Anglo Saxon beaver's tooth amulet, and an Indian gold amulet.

Room 62

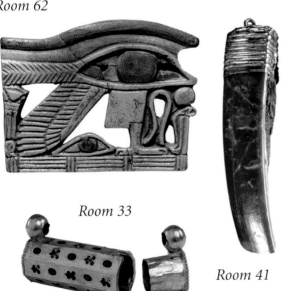

Room 33

Room 41

As well as individuals, families and whole communities try to protect themselves from danger. The inhabitants of the Nicobar Islands in the Indian Ocean used *kareau* figures like this one to drive off evil spirits and keep them away. Placed inside, the *kareau* would guard the family home. On duty at the entrance to the village it looked after everyone.

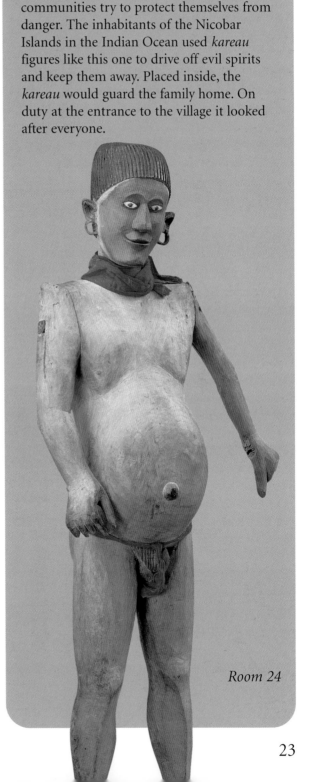

Room 24

6

The Turquoise Serpent

Where did it come from?

It is from Mexico, from the Aztec culture.

How old is it?

It was probably made in the 14th or 15th century AD before the arrival of the Spanish.

What is it made from?

It is carved from a piece of wood and then covered in mosaic pieces made mainly from turquoise with some red and white shell.

Who owned it?

It must have belonged to a very important person, perhaps even Motecuhzoma, the last ruler of the Aztecs.

What is it?

It may have been worn on the chest or head as part of a rich ceremonial costume, or it may have been fixed to the top of a pole and carried as an emblem of some sort.

Where can I see it?

It is in Room 27 – the Mexican Gallery – along with several other turquoise mosaics.

How was the serpent made?

The tiny pieces of turquoise and shell – called tesserae – were stuck to the wooden frame with resin. Recent research by the Museum's scientists has shown how carefully the tesserae were shaped and polished and how some of them had their sharp edges smoothed before being stuck on.

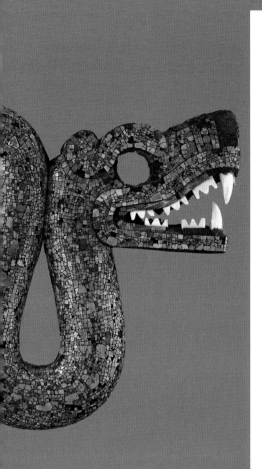

The Aztecs controlled a vast empire of about 20 million people in the region that is now Mexico, Guatemala, Belize and parts of Honduras and El Salvador. Tenochtitlan, a city built on an island in a lake, was the home of the Aztec ruler and of the most powerful noble families and officials and was also an important religious centre. Merchants, some of them women, lived in special areas of Tenochtitlan and organized trade all over the empire and beyond. One of the furthest regions with which the Aztecs traded was the southwest of what is now the USA, a thousand miles away, from where the Aztecs obtained the semi-precious stone called turquoise.

To the Aztecs, turquoise was more highly valued than gold. On this serpent the small, shiny mosaic pieces are like the scales of a snake's skin. But turquoise was more than just beautiful; it had a symbolic value as the blue of water. Water, Earth, Sky and Fire were vitally important elements: Water, in the form of rain and rivers, was the giver of life. Animals were also important symbols. The curves of the body and the quick movement of snakes were connected with the flow of water and the flash of lightning. Snakes shed their skin and so also stood for renewal and the cycle of Time.

In 1519 a Spanish army under the command of Hernan Cortes arrived in Mexico. Within two years, the Aztecs were defeated, their last ruler Motecuhzoma was dead and the city of Tenochtitlan was destroyed. For the majority of the native people of Mexico, Spanish rule was no better and often worse than Aztec rule. They were forced to work for their rulers, they paid increased tribute and many thousands died from diseases to which they had no resistance.

What happened to the Aztecs?

The Aztecs continued to live under Spanish rule and many of them kept their traditions alive, often combining Catholic beliefs with their old religious customs. Today, more than one and a quarter million people still speak Nahuatl, the language of the Aztecs, and many of them have beliefs and ways of life directly linked to their Aztec past.

Animals

Snakes were of huge importance to the Aztec people. All cultures have explored the relationship between humans and animals and there is not a room in the British Museum that is not home to at least one creature.

Room 10

These horses and their handsome young riders are part of the frieze that decorated the Parthenon in Athens – the most famous ancient Greek temple. Along with all the other sculptures on the building, they symbolize the democratic power of Athens. In the drawing by Edward Lear below, his horse and rider are very different as they frantically flee an attack by huge flies!

Room 18

This is another contrasting pair of animals. The ivory box from ancient Syria is in the form of a duck that turns to feed her ducklings, which are now missing. How different from the haughty peacock from Iran, who symbolizes beauty and sophisticated pleasure.

Room 57

Lions are familiar to us as symbols of the power of a king. These carvings (left) decorated the palace of a king of Assyria. The king shows his strength by hunting lions and also protects his people from danger. To us, the fight seems cruel and unfair as the lions have been brought to a special hunting ground in cages and cannot escape. The ancient viewer would not have felt the same.

This terrapin was probably made as a garden ornament for a Mughal emperor in what is now Pakistan. Imagine it standing near or in the cool waters of a fountain or pond. It is made of jade and is so accurate that we can even tell what species of terrapin it is – to find out, take the Terrapin Challenge at www.mughalindia.co.uk!

Room 34

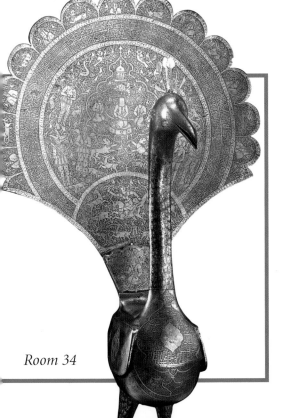

Room 34

Room 25

Kozo is a dog from the Kongo people of central Africa. He lives in the home, but hunts in the forests where the Kongo buried their dead, so he can move between the worlds of the living and of the dead. His two heads and four eyes make him powerful. The Kongo priest-doctor put strong medicines in the hole in his back and gave him messages and tasks by hammering strips of metal into his back.

7

The mummy of Nesperennub

What is it?

The body of an ancient Egyptian priest which was preserved by mummification. It is still inside its coffin.

How old is it?

Nesperennub lived about 800 BC.

Where did it come from?

The mummy was probably found in the tomb of Nesperennub's family, somewhere on the west bank of the Nile at Luxor (ancient Thebes).

Why is this mummy special?

One of the reasons is that he is a film star! Nesperennub was the subject of a special exhibition in 2004 called *Mummy: the inside story* which featured a 3-D film using the latest technology to let visitors take a journey inside the mummy itself.

Where can I see it?

Gallery 62 (when it returns from travelling around USA and Japan).

The surface of the cartonnage case is covered with paintings showing the gods who Nesperennub hoped would protect him and help him to enter his new life in the next world.

There are more than a hundred Egyptian mummies in the British Museum and this is one of the best preserved of them all. Nesperennub was a priest of the god Khons about 800 BC. When he died his body was embalmed and wrapped in linen bandages to preserve it for ever. Then the mummy was placed inside a special kind of coffin called a cartonnage case. It is made from many layers of cloth, glued together to form a body-shaped shell and then covered with fine plaster ready for painting.

By mummifying Nesperennub and putting him inside this case, the skilled craftsmen of ancient Egypt were making a new body for him – one that his spirit could live inside for ever. He hoped to enter the world of the gods, free from the kind of problems he might have known on earth, such as hunger, pain and discomfort.

The case has never been opened since the day it was sealed up almost 3,000 years ago. To find out what it contains it has been CT scanned in a hospital. The scans show Nesperennub's body very clearly. Pictures of the skull show that he had an illness that damaged the bone and may have left marks on his skin. The ancient Egyptians wanted to be always young and healthy in the afterlife. That is how Nesperennub is shown in the face on the cartonnage case. It does not show us Nesperennub as he really looked, but from the scans of his body we can build up a picture of his real face.

Reconstructed face of Nesperennub.

What are CT scans?

CT stands for 'computerized tomography'. It is widely used in modern medicine. It means that instead of taking one x-ray photograph, the machine takes lots and then puts them together using a computer to give a very highly detailed picture of the body from all directions.

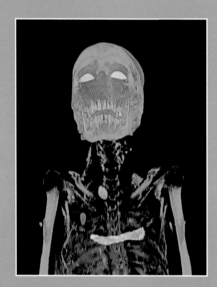

So how did he die?

We can tell from his skull and skeleton that Nesperennub was about forty when he died, which was quite a good age for ancient Egyptian men. Some features of his bones indicate that he was beginning to suffer from arthritis and that he experienced illness or malnutrition early in his life. His teeth were worn, but in reasonably good condition, although he had an abscess which must have caused him pain. The only clue to his death is a small hole in his skull which may be the result of a severe illness attacking the bone – it does not seem to be due to any violence.

Personal appearance

Computer technology allows us to see Nesperennub's face nearly three thousand years after his death. The British Museum is full of different faces, bodies and ways of dressing.

Room 33

South stairs

This Buddhist monk's fat belly stands for good luck and contentment – he has plenty to eat and can afford to laugh and smile with no fear of hunger. The ancient Greeks would not have thought much of his body shape. For them, the ideal man was fit and muscular and showed off his body by competing naked in athletics competitions.

These two images of women are from tombs. This is how their families wanted them to be remembered. The women look their best – neat hairstyles, fine dresses and veils and rich jewellery. Tamma (far left) is from Palmyra, a wealthy city in Syria. Seianti, an Etruscan from central Italy, holds a mirror to check her appearance. The Museum contains mirrors from all round the world showing that humans have always been interested in how they look.

Room 70

Room 71

Room 46

This man is clearly out to make an impression. His wig is curled into elaborate ringlets; he wears a wide lace collar, rich robes and the chain and medallion of the Order of the Garter. He is Prince Rupert, a general of the Royalists in the English Civil War.

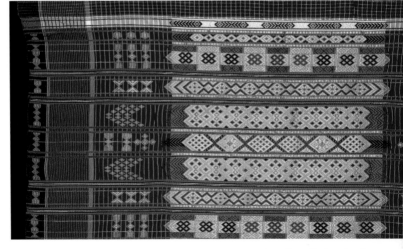

Room 25 (temporarily off display)

Throughout the Museum you will find pieces of jewellery to be worn on necks, fingers, toes, ankles, heads, noses and ears. Jewellery is often made from gold or silver, but you will find many other materials used too such as turquoise, glass, carnelian and coral.

Some clothes are made for special occasions. This *biskri* took several weeks to weave and would first be worn by a Tunisian bride as part of her wedding dress. It is about four metres long and is made from cotton. The intricate patterns are woven in silk or metal thread and all of them have names such as beans, rice, heart and chair. These show what is hoped for from the marriage: love, children and a peaceful home.

31

8

Otobo sculpture

What is it?

It's a sculpture of a man in a masquerade costume.

How old is it?

It was made in 1995.

Where did it come from?

It actually comes from London, but it shows a man from the Kalabari people of southern Nigeria.

Who made it?

It was made by the artist Sokari Douglas Camp, who was born in Nigeria but has been living and working in London for many years.

What is it made of?

It is made mostly of painted steel.

Where can I see it?

Room 25, the Sainsbury African Galleries, where you can also see many other objects connected with masquerade and a video of a masquerade performance.

An original wooden Otobo mask.

In the sculpture the man is wearing an Otobo or hippopotamus masquerade costume. We tend to think of hippos as rather gentle, cuddly creatures, but they are in fact very dangerous and frequently upset canoes in the region of the Niger Delta where the Kalabari live. Masquerade is one way of controlling the spirits of wild creatures such as the hippo and getting them to work for the good of society.

The wooden Otobo mask is worn on the top of the head looking upwards and is just one part of an elaborate costume which includes cloth, palm leaves, brushes, knives and rattles. Movement and music also have equal importance in the performance. The hippo masquerader responds to the complicated language of sounds and rhythms of the drummers with steps, hand gestures and head movements. Sometimes he even attacks spectators in line with his reputation as a fierce and dangerous creature.

As a woman, Sokari Douglas Camp would not be permitted to join the exclusively male society which enacts the Otobo masquerade; equally, she would not be permitted to work in metal, the main material used in the sculpture. Among the Kalabari, as in most traditional African societies, metalworking is only carried out by men. In the African galleries the Museum uses the work of modern African artists to provide new ways of looking at older traditions – the hippopotamus masquerade has been danced by the Kalabari for at least two hundred years.

As a contemporary artist, Sokari has added her modern views on these ancient traditions, providing us with food for thought as we look at her sculpture and its accompanying video, together with original elements of the masquerade costume.

Where else do you find masquerades?

Most parts of the world including Britain have festivals which involve the wearing of masks. On the northwest coast of North America, native people wear masks at ceremonies to mark important events in the community. In South America and elsewhere in the world, Carnival is a very popular events for masked dances and performances. On the left you can see a masquerade that takes place in Romania at New Year. The three 'Doctor' characters (above left) are taking a break – two of them have pushed their masks to the tops of their heads.

Music and dance

In the Sainsbury African Galleries you can see and hear a video of a real masquerade performance. The Museum's galleries are full of music and dance if you just let your imagination get to work.

Room 56

The citole was a medieval version of a guitar. The one below was altered several times over a period of more than two hundred years and may have been used to play songs of love at the court of Queen Elizabeth I. The lyre on the right was probably also played in a royal court, but nearly four thousand years earlier in the palace of one of the kings of Ur in modern-day Iraq.

Room 27

Room 2

Percussion instruments are probably the oldest type of musical instrument. You will find many examples of drums in the Museum. This pottery figure of a man playing a drum is from a tomb in Mexico.

Room 33

Room 61

Music and dance go together perfectly. Most of the dances you will find in the Museum are for religious rituals or special celebrations rather than for the sheer joy of dancing. The Indian god Shiva dances the dance of time – the sound of his drum calls in a new creation. The Egyptian women dance to pipes at a party, but here too there is probably a connection with new life, as the party was painted on the walls of a tomb. Even the three simple female figures from Greece, their hands joined in a circle, were probably an offering to a god.

Room 12

Temporarily off display

Room 25 (temporarily off display)

Wind instruments range from complicated trumpets to simple whistles. The horn of an animal made a good loud noise and was popular for hunting and warfare. The horn above is more than 5000 years old and comes from Europe. While it keeps the shape of a real horn, it is actually made of bronze. The figure of a musician from Benin in west Africa shows how to play it – by blowing through a side hole, not down the end.

9

Figures from a Chinese tomb

Where did they come from?

They are from Luoyang, in north central China.

How old are they?

They were made in AD 728 during the Tang Dynasty.

What are they made from?

The figures are made of earthenware pottery covered with a three-coloured glaze.

What are they?

They are tomb figures, made to accompany high-ranking individuals during their funeral and into the afterlife.

Why are they special?

These figures are among the tallest Tang tomb figures in existence.

Where can I see them?

They are in the middle of the Chinese section of the Asia Gallery (room 33).

A merchant caravan with camels on the Silk Road in the early 20th century.

These figures were originally displayed on carts as part of the funeral procession for General Liu Tingxun. Once the procession had arrived at the tomb, they were lined up outside. After the coffin had been put in the burial chamber, they were placed in their proper positions inside the tomb. The figures include two earth spirits to frighten away evil spirits, two Guardian Kings and two officials, one military (wearing a breastplate) and one civil – Liu Tingxun was both a military and civil official during his life. There are two camels and horses and their grooms. They remind us of the caravans or groups of traders and merchants that travelled the 'Silk Road', which prospered during the Tang Dynasty.

The Silk Road was a network of land and sea routes which connected China with the Mediterranean 5,000 miles away. The eastern part of the Silk Road began in the city of Xi'an. It then passed across the deserts of western China and through cities such as Tashkent and Samarkand in central Asia. At the western end, the routes passed through Iran and Iraq into Syria and then to Rome in the west and Egypt in the south. Few caravans went all the way from China to the Mediterranean – Greek, Arab, Roman, Iranian, and Indian traders exchanged goods with nomads in central Asia, who in turn handed over to the Chinese further east.

As well as silk, the caravans carried to the west jade, steel and farming equipment and manufactured goods made of lacquer and bamboo. China imported exotic spices and perfumes, thoroughbred horses and jewels. Technological inventions and ideas including printing, gunpowder and the compass spread from China across the continents of Europe, Asia and Africa. Many artistic influences – Greek, Iranian, Indian and Chinese – travelled along the Silk Road and in the period of the Tang Dynasty, Xi'an was home to thousands of foreigners from all over the world.

What was the Tang Dynasty?

The emperors who ruled China from AD 618 to AD 906 called their dynasty Tang. In general, the Tang emperors ruled firmly and fairly and China grew wealthy and powerful. Trade brought in goods, raw materials and influences from other parts of the world and the arts and poetry flourished. Many believe that this was the most glorious period in Chinese history.

What is special about the horses?

In the second and first centuries BC, the Chinese grew to admire the tall powerful horses from Ferghana, a region of Central Asia spreading across eastern Uzbekistan, Tajikistan and Kyrgyzstan. These horses were far superior to their own small ponies, especially in battles against the nomadic peoples on the borders of the Empire. Their desire for these so-called 'heavenly horses' was one of the factors leading to the development of the Silk Road. Eventually, the Chinese bought enough of the horses to be able to breed them themselves.

Travel and transport

The Silk Road along which the camel trains travelled carried goods, people, ideas and influences from one place to another. The British Museum shows all the cultures of the world in contact with each other.

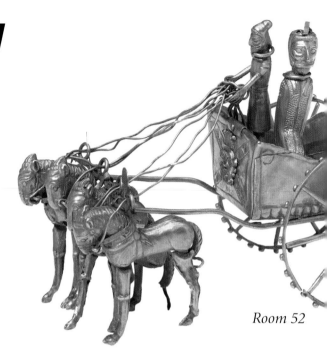

Room 52

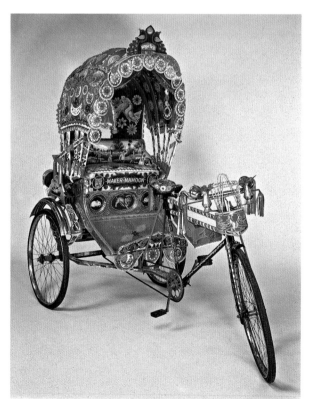

(temporarily off display)   Room 26

The bright colours and lively pictures that decorate this 20th century tricycle rickshaw from Bangladesh (left) transform it from an ordinary vehicle into a fantastic object of beauty. In this way it is not that far from the stately model chariot made of solid gold (above) from the ancient Persian Empire which was made more than two thousand years ago. The sled below may not be as magnificent, but was made with equal care from the natural resources available to the Inuit people of Greenland – it is made from bone and walrus ivory with a little wood and is tied together with walrus skin.

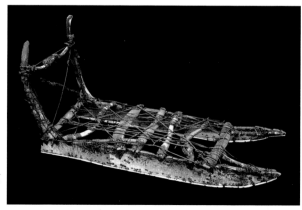

Trade and travel bring people in contact with each other. The kingdom of Benin in what is now Nigeria was a sophisticated, confident society ruled by a powerful Oba (king). The Portuguese first set up links with Benin in the 1460s and 1470s trading coral beads, guns and brass for pepper, cloth, ivory and slaves. A Benin ivory carver made this salt cellar in the late 1500s. It shows Europeans through the eyes of a different culture.

Room 38

Room 25

Amazingly, this ship is a clock which can roll along a dinner table, play music, fire cannons and … tell you the time. It was made in Germany in 1585 in the form of a European ship like those which at just that time were sailing the world's oceans in pursuit of natural resources, trade, wealth and power. In the 1590s more than 2,700 tonnes of silver arrived in Europe from the New World of the Americas, most of it on Spanish ships. The 8-reales coins below are made of silver from South America – the famous 'pieces of eight' for which pirates had such a longing.

Keep exploring

Would you like to read more about the objects in the British Museum and the people who made them? Here are some suggestions.
You can find these British Museum books, and many more, in the British Museum shops or online at www.britishmuseum.org/shop

500 Things to Know About the Ancient World, Carolyn Howitt

African Crafts, Lynne Garner

The Ancient Egyptians: Their Lives and Their World, Angela McDonald

The Ancient Greeks: Their Lives and Their World, Alexandra Villing

The Ancient Romans: Their Lives and Their World: Paul Roberts

Colouring Book of Ancient Britain: Celtic Iron Age, Roman Britain, Anglo-Saxons, Vikings

Pocket Dictionary Ancient Egyptian Mummies, Nigel Strudwick

Pocket Dictionary Aztec and Maya Gods and Goddesses, Clara Bezanilla

Pocket Dictionary Roman Emperors, Paul Roberts

Pocket Guide to Egyptian Hieroglyphs, Richard Parkinson

Pocket Timeline of Ancient Mesopotamia, Katharine Wiltshire

Pocket Timeline of China, Jessica Harrison-Hall

Pocket Timeline of Islamic Civilizations, Nicholas Badcott

The Story of Writing, Carol Donoughue

Richard Woff is Head of Schools and Young Audiences at the British Museum. He is the author of several books for children.

Thanks are due to the following British Museum curators who wrote contributions and acted as consultants:

Lissant Bolton	Colin McEwan	Chris Spring
Ben Burt	Richard Parkinson	John Taylor
Mary Ginsberg	James Robinson	Alexandra Villing
Sonja Marzinzik	Keith Southwell	

© 2007 The Trustees of the British Museum

First published by British Museum Press
A division of The British Museum
Company Ltd
38 Russell Square, London WC1B 3QQ
britishmuseum.org/publishing

Tenth impression 2012

ISBN: 978-0-7141-3032-3

Richard Woff has asserted his right to be identified as the author of this work
A catalogue record for this title is available from the British Library

Designed and typeset by Turchini Design
Printed and bound in Italy by Printer Trento, Trento

Illustration acknowledgements

All photographs were taken by members of the British Museum Department of Photography and Imaging and are © The Trustees of the British Museum unless otherwise stated below.

Page 24 bottom: Courtesy of Fulmar Television and Film Ltd.

Page 29 CT scan: © Photographic imagery courtesy of SGI.

Page 29 head of Nebamun: Facial reconstruction by Dr Caroline Wilkinson, The University of Manchester.

Page 33 bottom: photos Sarah Posey, Keeper of World Art, Royal Pavilion, Libraries and Museums, Brighton & Hove.

Page 36 merchant caravan: British Library.